whiskey words & a shovel III

whiskey words & a shovel III

r.h. Sin

Andrews McMeel
PUBLISHING®

beneath everything.

love me to the bone

beneath the nerves

beyond my mistakes

beneath my veins

and even as my heart breaks

love me entirely

or not at all

my own stranger.

broken mirrors

keepers of my reflection

shards of glass

on the bathroom floor

I don't recognize

my own self

my own eyes

look like those of a stranger

as my confusion

stares back at me

trying to make sense of it all

I am a stranger to myself

nightfall.

the perfect distraction from the stars
she made the moon look dull
she kept the sky lit each night

laws in love.

despite it all

she's brave enough

to love you

reward her with affection

reward her with your loyalty

and truth

in the dark.

I'm hiding behind this smile
and lately
chaos has found its way
into my heart
there's a shade of gray
that covers my day to day
and fills me with the type
of sadness
difficult to define with words

the darkness hovers over me
like vultures awaiting supper
ever so patiently
as life takes a toll on my soul

nearly out of my mind

and out of control

searching for myself

in mirrors

yet all I see

is a face that I don't know

who am I

and if I were to lose

this fight

where in the hell

would I go

wrong for trying.

just because you choose a person
doesn't mean they're right for you
just because you love a person
doesn't mean they're the one for you

so much of what we feel for someone
can be so one-sided and yet we think
that if we give that person
more than they deserve
that somehow it'll change
the way they feel about us

affirmation.

you are good enough

you are worthy

you are strong

you are beautiful

it's not your fault

good things are coming

you are so important

you can't give up now

you just need to let him go

you have to stop beating yourself up

forgive yourself for staying longer

than you should have

you can't blame yourself

yes, this is a sign

yes, I'm talking to you

life-aches.

the plan was to get better

but there are demons

at every level

the moment you feel like

you've won

you then realize that the more you
advance

the more you have to lose

and nothing ever gets easier

you just learn better ways

to navigate a life that seemingly

becomes tougher

last year I had nothing

and the emptiness was expected

this year I have more

but the emptiness

continues to haunt me

life is a complex thing

that can't be solved with things

and maybe I'm beginning to realize

the unimportance of material items

maybe the toughness of it all

is making me stronger

the only one.

genuine love, something real

something to cherish

something worth fighting for

in a world filled with women

I hope you find someone

who isn't afraid to commit

to a relationship with just you

better.

you invested so much

of yourself into him

and the way

he should've felt for you

is the way he's chosen

to feel for someone else

but you'll be fine

and you'll find something better

be strong

consilium I.

the love you deserve

can't be found

while holding on to someone

who doesn't deserve you

July 18th 2016.

there are so many firsts
that I'd like to experience
with you and only you

I often felt that I was
always wasting my time
but energy invested in you
in us, is time well spent
with someone who will always
be worth it

savage.

it's not always pretty
and she's not always
this picture-perfect bullshit
definition of what's considered
to be beautiful
but that's a woman
someone capable of becoming
whatever she needs to be
whenever she needs to be it

sometimes she's a savage
but only when appropriate
an alpha among the wolves
and when shit gets tough
whenever her life becomes
a war zone
she straps up her fucking boots
and goes to war
she fights, she's always been a fighter

found.

in silence, we discover ourselves

between the cracks.

she has twisted, dark,

and painful stories crammed

between the cracks in her heart

scattered across the surface of her
own soul

stay with her and listen

she's worth it

she's always been worth it

your past.

I shouldn't be bothered
by the things that happened
before me, before us

and I know that your past
belongs only to you
but it's your demons
that keep me awake at night

as I search for some sort
of emotional relief
under the moon in the darkness

after life.

I've been dying to stay alive

I've been dying to survive you

Gods.

good women are Godly

to Samantha.

I'm not perfect

I have many flaws

and you put up with me

regardless

in appreciation for all

that you do

and all that you represent in my life

I give you my truth and my loyalty

I give you my effort and my time

I love everything about you

the way you squint your eyes

and smile when you're genuinely happy

the way you show concern

and care for those who are close to
your heart

and your strength

there is nothing more beautiful than
a woman

who continues to fight

despite the chaos and madness

that surrounds her

in more ways than one

I admire you, my love

722 our love.

she asks for nothing

and so I plan to give her everything

2011.

I woke up one night

in a cold sweat, a nightmare perhaps

I don't really recall or maybe

I just didn't remember

maybe I didn't want to

there was still this sense of fear

surrounding me

I was in a dark place at the time

thinking that I was in love

when truly, I was in hell

regret for breakfast then dinner

starving for something real

holding on to someone who proved

to be fraudulent

most nights I felt empty

desperate to feel something other
than pain

exchanging my moral code for pleasure

but as soon as I'd cum

I'd also come to my senses

I wanted more, not only did I need more

but I deserved it

see, I'd given all of myself

to someone who eventually gave me
nothing

and I didn't realize it until the end

of the fucked-up situation

that I regretfully called a
relationship

I chose partners based on the way

I felt about myself

and I could only find and appreciate

something real after

loving myself more

the realization.

slowly it begins

you never really see it coming

and before you know it

everything you thought was real

turns out to be some majestic lie

some great big lie

that you believed

because within that lie

lived all the things you wanted to hear

all the fucking things you needed

to be told to you

by the lips of someone

who never really cared for you

in the first place

your heart confused

as your mind then takes on

the task of going to war

with the emotions you cultivated

based on the words

of someone who never meant

the things they said

separation.

broken down by solitude

separated by the silence

she was and still is everything.

she could replace the sun

if she wanted to

because nothing shined brighter

than when she smiled

she was love

and I was ready

for the light

that lived within her

one cold summer.

I was just thinking
or mentally screaming
scratching at the walls
of my own mind

yesterday
you claimed to love me
but today
feels more like hatred

I now find myself
searching for what we were
I'm currently avoiding
the truth in what we've become

so cold

so empty

so numb and detached

why does love

feel like death

a relationship

turned funeral

day to day.

one day it won't hurt as much

as it does now

sometime in the near future

day to day

it'll get easier

the nights won't feel so lonely

the mornings won't be so damn difficult

your heart may ache now

but there's power in pain

and you're just getting stronger

understand.

you must understand this
a man will never appreciate
your love
until he begins
to value his own

he will never love you entirely
until he begins to love himself

break us.

sometimes we give them too much credit

sometimes we overexaggerate their power

sometimes they don't really break you

maybe you simply break yourself

by trying to hold on to them

garden.

her heart is a garden

filled with dead roses

and weeds

from seeds planted

by those who left

these lives matter I.

I'm hurting because
the color of my skin
makes me perfect
for their target practice

I'm hurting because
in killing them
they're killing me

anger, then nothing.

my blood is boiling
my eyes have begun to water
as my voice begins to crack
my hands slowly shake
and so I place them to my sides

it's overwhelming
this has been so overwhelming
and difficult

I am so quick to anger
I blacked out once
thank the heavens
for keeping me
in every moment I've lost myself

I'm searching for the words

but silence fills me

like air

but the air in my lungs

has begun to escape me

and I fear that in moments

there will be nothing left

false friendship.

friendship is a lost art

the very word

has lost its true meaning

two people

wasting each other's energy

disguising hatred

with love

masking deceit with fun

and then it crumbles

time begins to test it

and it fails

vs.

she was trying to walk away

and hold on

at the same time

that's the mind at war

with the heart

please keep fighting.

you couldn't keep her down

in the midst of feeling broken

the victim

became the fighter

departed.

when silence is

the only answer

it's over

most hurtful.

I think what hurts the most
is knowing the moments of tomorrow
may never come

and so in the present
you find yourself making time
for someone who
can barely find the time for you

I think what hurts the most
is preserving your energy
for someone who would rather
invest their energy into something
other than the moments you've vacated
just to make room for them

time is something we find ourselves
taking for granted
time is something
we often think we have
until there is no time left to spend

I think what hurts the most
is the time we invest
in people who refuse to invest
that time back

only after.

you were never as important

to them

as you thought

and that's what hurts

that's what makes you

shut down

and shut others out

cultivate.

if what you love

causes you pain

let it go

and create your own peace

May 11th.

he doesn't miss you
he only sent that text
because he was horny
or lonely
possibly bored

see, weak men
know what to say
to get a woman's heart going
her mind racing
overthinking

he doesn't miss you
maybe the woman
he left you for
has upset him
maybe he's just bored
with something new
and in that moment
he's ready to exchange it
for something familiar

remember how it was before

remember how he left you

in the middle of that emotional storm

the storm that nearly destroyed you

and now here you are

happiness on the horizon

hands scarred from picking up

the shreds of your own existence

you're almost there

you whisper to your own heart

you're nearly there

peace is within reach

your phone lights up

and it's him

you have a choice . . .

choose yourself

some change.

and you're so used

to being mistreated

that anything opposite

of what you're used to

scares you

even if it's what you deserve

dear Mr. King.

with the mind-set of a King

you raised the princess

that became my Queen

and I love you for that

cloaked.

she buried her own sadness
under the weight of her smile
she buried most of her pain
in a box cloaked by her silence

and she's reading this now . . .

fed up.

more and more
you begin to value
all of what you have to offer
you become less likely
to share yourself with those
who don't deserve your time

your tolerance for bullshit
is now at an all-time low

therapy by the books.

deep halls

with books on both ends

I've buried so much of what I felt

into the pages of my favorite book

sadness slowly fading

with each chapter I read

my screams silenced

by words that resonate with my soul

a resting place for the words of authors

who seem to understand me more

than my own family and friends

the library is therapy

for those with minds like mine

vitae.

made wiser with heartache

made stronger by pain

absence and peace II.

the chaos left with you
providing a space for peace . . .

it all begins the same
different people
in similar situations
dealing with a pain
that is identical

strangers attempting to survive
the same type of incidents

emotional anguish and stress
psychological pain
the aches of a heart
riddled with cracks
weighed down by betrayal

there's a type of emptiness
that fills the soul
with the departure
of anyone you thought you loved

weird isn't it
that you can be filled
with the right type of emptiness

the type of emptiness
that leaves a space
or opportunity for something good
to take up residence

all in all
some of what you lose
gives you a chance
to gain something better

in order to discover peace
absence is needed

want, desire, lust.

being wanted is not enough

desire is mostly bullshit

lust is subpar

and oftentimes giving in

means giving up

the best parts of your existence

to those who will later treat you

as if you don't exist

the same ones who want you

may also intend to hurt you

it's never really apparent

until the end

friends become enemies

lovers start to feel like strangers

and there's nothing strange about it

it's not enough to be wanted

fuck desire, fuck temptation

preserve yourself for those

who deserve you

love and emptiness.

she saw love in empty hearts
constantly feeling for someone
incapable of feeling for her

that's the saddest part of love
being there alone

April 22nd.

she has passion
a reckless devotion
a loyalty that's unbreakable
and a truth that's unapologetic

she is love in the deepest form
so beautiful, extremely rare

she is everything she needs to be
in search of all that she deserves
she is you

rebuilt.

the beauty in breaking
is that when you rebuild
you'll be stronger than before

the absence.

even while married

she felt alone

he was there

but fully unavailable

midnight Colorado.

maybe we should have

left earlier

the darkness of the night

attacked the sky

with so much precision

fatigue could've been

my enemy

the way it crept up on me

without warning

I was tired

and so were you

those brown eyes

slightly covered

as your eyelids

gave way to the night

with a pit in my stomach

we drove off into the darkness

but I was brave

because you were next to me

stale.

the mornings

were no longer good

and so we stopped

greeting each other

silence became

our language

tension was our communication

between the lack of dialogue

and the arguments

when we did speak

something broke

we simply shattered

we were destined

for the end

left wondering

why the fuck we even began

in the first place

strange love.

I hope you find someone
who falls in love with the strange
that lives within you

a silent thought.

you're always hurting me

and yet I'm always the one apologizing

under the veil.

the saddest souls

seem the happiest

I see your smile

I hear your laughter

and yet, I feel your pain

hell of a woman.

chariots could fly

upon your whispers

the ocean made calm

by the sound of your voice

chaos transformed into peace

because of your presence

one hell of a woman

with heaven in her smile

the woman I love.

the wind whispers

her name

and the sun rises

early enough

just to witness

the opening of her eyes

she is love

trapped in human skin

she is love

in the form of a woman

te amo.

I love you
and what that means
is that I promise
to be better than what you've had
I promise to give you something
that is completely different
than what you've known

a reason why.

it's true

isn't it . . .

you hold on to a person

who creates chaos in your heart

because they weren't always like that

and you figure that staying around
long enough

gives them an opportunity to change

but here's the fucking truth . . .

they won't

today then tomorrow.

choosing myself is the most obvious
choice

and yet it has become the hardest thing

I've ever had to do

going back and forth with my decision to
leave

so hard on myself

based on that decision, my future unclear

it's scary not knowing

what tomorrow will look like

but it's terrifying

knowing that I'll waste another day

trying to love the unlovable

the very predictable

the inconsiderate, you

sour nothings.

sleep, dear, he's no longer worth it

722, in love with my best friend.

it's so important to find someone

you always want to be around

and I always want to be with her

I can't imagine a life

where my mornings

don't begin with her waking eyes

that provide me with some sense

of hope that love is real

I don't want to imagine a life

where my peace

isn't dependent on her presence

I trust my ups and downs

in the palms of her hands

and I'm overjoyed

to experience a world

where we've found each other

the self-hate.

because that's what it usually is
and that's how it'll always be

the way they treat you
represents their own truth
and mistreating others
is symbolic of self-hatred

with that being said
I forgive you
for not loving yourself
enough to appreciate me

wasting time, making time.

the painful truth

is that you're constantly

trying to spend your life

with someone who won't even

give you a fucking moment

of their day

you've been trying

to create a future

with someone who belongs

to your past

and you've been hurting yourself

by doing so

lost out here.

and here you are
a slave to your own sadness
subjecting yourself to disrespect
self-medicating with alcohol and sex

all based upon the mistreatment
of someone who failed to love you
putting yourself at risk
every time you let them touch you

conversations with good women.

and she told me he loved her
then proceeded to tell how often
he'd fuck other women
several times, more than once

I think it's fucked up that she accepted
the type of shit
that would eventually
destroy her in the end

she stayed because of a love
that was never really there

good book.

a good book is something
you can reread over and over
yet it never loses its intrigue
that's the type of love I want
that's the type of love I deserve

used to it.

you're so used to being hurt

that you don't know how to

allow real love in

you're so used to the heartache

that your heart anticipates being
broken

you're so damn used to the lies

that even the truth appears to be
unbelievable

beautiful savage.

she was a beautiful savage
unapologetic but sweet
delicate but tough
brave enough
to walk through hell
in search of her own piece
of heaven
unafraid of the flames
determined to survive
through the things
meant to destroy her

she had the mental strength

of a warrior

as she continued to run wild

on those who attempted to cage

her ambition

she was whatever she wanted to be

she went wherever she wanted to go

in pursuit of freedom

in pursuit of love

in pursuit of herself

fuck those articles
in female magazines.

maybe if you fuck him this way

he'll be faithful

maybe if you dress like this

he'll pay more attention to you

maybe if you change yourself

you'll change his mind

maybe if you try harder

he'll make an effort

the truth is

you can't keep a man

who doesn't deserve to keep you

fuck any article that tells you

how to keep a man

by making it seem as if you're the
problem

you're not . . .

beyond her surface.

compliment her thoughts

value a woman's mind

see beyond your eyesight

feel beneath the surface

every day.

at the end of every day
a woman just wants to feel loved
by the man she loves

it's as simple as that
it's not being needy
it's being deserving

the lie that is love.

most of what we know

about love

has been defined

by a lifetime of mistrust

and disappointment

most of what we know

about love

has been taught

by individuals

who only encouraged our pain

we paint the walls

of our mind

in white

to hide the dirt and the cracks

we suppress the pain of it all

with good memories

slightly exaggerated

to create this picture

too large for its frame

we want love

but we accept hate

we invest energy

into those

who rarely make an effort

we display emotional anguish

in the form of yelling

toward someone who doesn't

even care to listen

most of what we know

about love is a lie

without permission.

eyes burning, heart sinking
innocence left in ruine
ruined by someone she trusted

what part of no
sounds like yes
blurred lines
and no consent

left aching
with the realization
that this will be something
she never forgets
something she wants to suppress

a nightmare, a living nightmare
wide awake, nowhere is safe
suffering in silence
always hurting but she won't say

April 18th.

I hope you fall in love
with someone
who hates the same things
as you do

I hope you fall for someone
who understands
why you feel the way
you feel
about certain things
and people

into the night.

I collapse into the night
under the pressure
of my own unhappiness
overthinking
pushing myself further
into the darkest corners
of my own existence

I've been smiling
in an attempt to avoid their concern
while trying to learn
to navigate through the chaos
that plagues my life

though genuine laughter
is what I've been after
I've been unable to find it
and so I resort to a cheerfulness
that isn't real
the type of joy
I only wish to feel

there is sadness all around us
it follows and swallows us up
us being the people like me

dreading tomorrow and the sorrows
that live within the minutes
of every passing moment

this has become my life
the life of someone who
in a room filled with others
still feels lonely

departure.

you were always the sadness

that I had to let go of

I lost you

and gained a necessary peace

freshman.

college destroyed

whatever innocence she had left

between the nights she couldn't remember

and the things she wished to forget

she'd forever be changed

by the events

that stripped away the peace from her
soul

girls like you I.

the girls

with the biggest smiles

have the saddest stories

hurt.

she did everything

he asked

she gave him everything

she had

and he gave what she deserved

to someone else

a struggle of mine.

it's only human, you know

sometimes we don't see things

for what they truly are

we see things for what

we want them to be

and this has been my struggle lately

when you want love

you see it in everything

even when it isn't there

poetry.

she's a badass

that makes her poetry

consilium II.

if he doesn't want a relationship

don't give him relationship benefits

scarlet love.

pics depicting nudity

in place of words

suggestive and subliminal

it's late

the moon sits alone in darkness

like you

like us

we meet here

to fill each other's void

though in different places

the feelings are mutual

staring into the viewfinder

the screen of my laptop

displays you like moving art

emotions in motion

as you curl then arch

I'm in awe of the artistry

your canvas, your figure

miles away but right in front of me

can't touch but we feel each other

my eyes like heavy palms

resting on your waist

as I watch you

you watch me . . .

wish you were here

self-talk.

some of the most honest conversations

I've ever had

were in a room

occupied by just me and my own voice

name the moon after her.

in more ways than one
she's like the moon
the light within her
shines in complete darkness

she's a shade of beauty
among the stars

truth in motion.

ignore the excuses

their actions

are their truth

flow.

it came unexpectedly
a river of red beginning to flow
and he's angry
because of the possibility of no sex

don't feel bad
for what comes naturally
don't apologize
for being a woman

August thoughts.

you don't deserve a lukewarm love

days and nights.

we struggle

we fight

hopeless days

sleepless nights

who you are.

you're one of those women

who thinks she's too hard to love

your guard is up

your trust issues at an all-time high

because the pursuit of love

has brought you nothing but pain

you just want to feel nothing

and you numb yourself

by hiding your heart behind the wall

you've built out of mistrust

and disappointment

you're the woman still trying

to piece herself back together

and even so

you're still the type of woman

deserving of a love that helps

you grow

you still deserve a love that feels

like the love you've always

been capable of providing

simple complications.

simple things

will always be made

to appear complicated

by the people who are too lazy

to make an effort

love is a simple gesture

complicated only when

directed toward someone

too lazy to reciprocate it

remember this . . .

sadly lying to myself.

I lied
I never loved you
couldn't trust you

you once helped me forget
but now you're just a reminder
a lonely reminder of what happens
when energy is misplaced
and invested into the wrong person

I was in search of love
and you were just the lie
I told myself
to keep from feeling alone
but there's been this void
in my heart
and I'm no longer using you
to fill it

core beliefs.

the belief that you
are not good enough
will force you
to entertain things
that are not worthy
of your time

the belief that you
are not good enough
will force you
to remain in an environment
that will destroy your ability
to thrive in any relationship
you attempt to create

the belief that you

are not good enough

will force you into situations

that will cause you

to compromise your standards

the belief that you

are not good enough

will keep you from

receiving the type of love

you deserve

new story.

you lost her

I love her

generational curse.

we've become a generation
so good at pretending to be happy
that we've lost the desire
to actually create true happiness

absence, you.

there's someone else
where you used to be
your replacement
is fully equipped
with everything you were lacking
and everything you denied me of

the memory of you, of us
no longer hurts me
because I no longer have
the capacity to feel pain

now, overcrowded
and overflowing with peace
because I discovered
the missing piece to my puzzle
in your absence

valid questions.

you fight but who fights for you

you love but who's loving you

your reflection.

I think she looked

into the mirror

and saw someone

worthy of the love

she wasted on others

torches.

burn bridges if you have to

don't be afraid of the flames

use the fire as warmth

use the fire as a torch

to light the path toward

something better

with someone better

pain is silent.

the worst type of pain is silent
and it hides behind a smile
upon the face of the strongest people

the heart, the lessons.

the heart has to break several times
in order to find hands
strong enough to hold it

this is what life has taught me
and it's been one of the hardest
lessons to learn

in order to find love
you must navigate successfully
through hate

lacrimae.

use your tears

to drown your demons

under the moon.

there were always those nights

when her mind went to war with her heart

the fight between what she knew

what she felt

and what she had to do

sometimes the hardest decisions

were made under the moon

unhappily happy.

we self-medicate using smiles and
laughter

a similar battle.

different people

in different places

upon earth

feeling some of the same things

battling some of the same demons

unshakable.

give me a love

that isn't shaken

by an argument

or disagreement

give me a love

that doesn't die

because of time

July 9th 2014.

understand this

read these words

and let them sink into

the depths of your heart

when a man ignores you

that doesn't mean try harder

it means do better

it means that your energy

is best served elsewhere

her guard.

you criticize her

for having a wall up

you persuaded her

to take her guard down

then you did exactly

what she feared you'd do

fuck you

for hurting the heart

of a woman

whom you never intended

to love

fuck you for making promises

you had no intention of keeping

fuck you

for lying about who you were

in order to get what you wanted

I want what you took for granted.

send her to me broken
and I'll love every piece of her existence

send her to me broken . . .
I'll help her forget about you
and all the fucking misfortunes you caused

the only thing wrong with a woman
whose heart is filled with pain
is the fact that she deserves the pleasure
and security that comes from loving
the right person

and I'd like that person to be me . . .

a chance.

be patient

be kind

be understanding

I am worth it

chasing midnight.

I've been so tired
from chasing sleep
while running away
from all of my problems

lost love in solitude.

I'm writing this
because it's difficult
to speak to you

my words either go
unheard or misinterpreted

I keep blaming myself
for your inability to process
the things I've expressed

I keep hurting myself
listening to your lies
and pretending to be happy
with a smile on my face
and pain in my heart

I'm writing this
as my heart hardens
and my soul screams

there's this eerie silence
surrounding me
as I let these words out
and I sit within these four walls
I'm beginning to feel free
I'm beginning to feel like me again

in losing you
I'll discover me

she, the journey.

she hid so much of what lived
within her heart
behind a smile that at times
appeared to be failing

she built her expectations
on pillars of lies
that at first gave off
the appearance of truth

laughter became a way
of drowning out the silence
that would sometimes
remind her of the things
she'd struggle to forget

but even in her darkest moments
she provided her own light
she became whatever she needed to be
in order to get closer
to a love she deserved

April 30th.

tonight we won't speak

our room filled with silence

only after the tension

that exploded into hurtful dialogue

I'm not listening

speaking over you

because you make me feel

as if my only place is beneath you

emotions bottled up

until the glass breaks

I spill my inner thoughts

across the walls

back and forth until

there's nothing left

falling asleep

eager to see if tomorrow

we'll be better

reached the bottom.

I'll be honest with you
whatever I felt has faded
into the air
or possibly it has sunk
to the bottom of the sea

drowning, always drowning
until I lost the will to fight
no longer able to see the surface
or the purpose of continuing
to fight for us

I'm done, it's over, the end

waiting for that text.

woke up

and the first thing I did

was check my phone

for a message

that wasn't there

the afternoon approaches

and still nothing

it's almost 4 p.m.

my fingers fumble

as I attempt to create a text

nothing profound

something simple

with much difficulty

erasing what I wrote

anxious, overthinking

putting my phone away

reluctantly

the moon is out now

as the darkness hides the sun

and still nothing

and now I feel like nothing

someone feeling something

for someone who feels nothing

or not enough

to be concerned with

whether or not we communicate

waiting for something that won't happen

losing sleep over someone

who sleeps peacefully

and what hurts the most

is that tomorrow it'll begin again

this feeling is never ending

this cycle is destructive

be still.

sweetheart, remain still

and be patient

you'll never have to chase

someone who wants to stay

you'll never need to compete

for the time

of someone who thinks

you're important

if they want you

they'll make an effort

if they love you

they'll show you

the loyal, the honest.

loyal souls know betrayal

better than anyone

the most honest souls

have been victim

to the worst lies

and the prettiest of hearts

have been through the ugliest shit

all in the name of love

good mourning.

wake up

hurting

uncertainty

stressed

depressed

guarded

unhappy

unable to find peace

unable to find joy

unable to find yourself

or your reflection

in the mirror

wake up

feeling hurt

you're uncertain

there's stress within you

depression now lives

in your soul

your guard is up

as you naturally feel this need

to protect yourself from something

or someone, them

you've lost your smile

your peace of mind compromised

and the joy of what you knew

has left you

you've been losing yourself

you can barely recognize

your own eyes as you stare

into the mirror

that's not love

you're not in love

and they don't love you

remember this

falling loving fighting.

falling for someone

doesn't mean they'll catch you

loving someone

doesn't make them deserve you

fighting for someone

won't make a difference

if that individual

doesn't appreciate you

don't waste yourself

on someone

who obviously wants someone else

a beautiful mess.

messy and imperfect but beautiful

your love

for the restless ones.

if you're unable to sleep

because of the shit

they put you through

then they're not worth it

pain by patience I.

just because she's patient
doesn't mean you should
make her wait

she is you IV.

and she was driven

by all the things

that caused her pain

as what failed to weaken her flames

became fuel

growing pains.

I spent my early 20s
searching for love
without knowing what
I was actually in search of

feeling things unexplainable
but never substantial
an emotion that seemed to escape me
whenever I thought my grip
was tight enough to keep it

but I didn't
I could never really love
because as it turns out
I didn't even know
how to love myself

what occurs.

one of two things

will occur when they're gone

you'll either realize

they were never there

or the fact that they're gone

doesn't even matter

because some people

are not a loss

ode to Samantha.

oh Samantha, my Samantha

my reason for hope

my definition of love

all I need, capable of providing

the love I deserve

your presence means so much to me

your touch places me on a cloud

higher than nine

and now I'm fine

mind lost in transition

as we move freely in our emotions

oh Samantha, my Samantha

I love you

halfway there.

though darkness
still fills the room
within my heart

I am less sad
when lying next to you

cleanse.

detach from what destroys you

evolving.

stop trying to save her

stop trying to change her

love a woman for who she is

and witness her evolve

into everything

she's supposed to be

she was grand.

the flowers envied her
and so did the sun
so rare, so beautiful

a grand representation
of what a woman should always be
though some claimed she was damaged
she meant everything to me

self-punishing attitudes.

you can't keep punishing yourself

for his inability

to live up to the promises

he made to your heart

it's not your fault . . .

wish, pray, or hope.

I hope you find the strength
to walk away from your past
and run toward a future
where you'll be treated
like the amazing soul that you are

I know life is short
and our moment here is limited
there's not enough time
to find all the things you want
but I do hope that you reach
all the things your heart deserves

romanticizing abandonment.

there is nothing romantic about someone

who takes all that you give them

and walks away as if

you meant nothing

only to return to you

to confess their love

after they've lost you

listen and understand

that you deserve someone

who enters your life

and stays

no matter how tough life gets

July 22nd reminds me.

you're the missing lyrics

to the song that lives within my soul

714.

nervousness subdued

while holding you

anxiety dissipates

as you smile

who knew this child

would be the cure

your head against my chest

listening to the quiet storm

that is my heartbeat

my peace now lives

in our moments together

as your existence

continues to build bridges

toward joy

so small

but so great

a minor

but major

and even though

I'm holding you

you're actually carrying me

love and its many ways to die.

the death of many relationships

lies in the hands of those

who would rather

hold on to mobile devices

than the hand of a lover

a sober realization.

I thought it was love
and so I allowed myself
to be deceived
by all the things
you helped me feel

fully fatigued.

so very tired of fighting, the end

October 25th 2015.

there's a certain level of peace

that comes with loving the right person

you feel safe and secure in their
presence

because you know that in a world filled

with uncertainty

you can always count on that certain
someone

to just be there

I've learned so much about love from you

and I'm grateful for the opportunity

to grow more in love with all that you
are

nothing is perfect

people aren't perfect but the fact that
you try

you always make an effort and continue
to go out

of your way to show me love

is simply proof that you are perfect
for me

be with someone who shows you that you
deserve

better than what you've had

turned off.

I can love you with my entire heart
yet walk away and ignore
your entire existence if you betray me
in a way I deem unacceptable

that's what happens
when you love yourself more
than the bullshit and lies
others attempt to feed you

after being hurt enough
your emotions become
something like a light switch
and once I'm turned off, that's it

a garden for Gods.

orange ground

beneath my feet

hand in hand

with my lover

surrounded by rocks

covered by blue skies

holding hawks

by their wings

listening to nature

say things

that only the soul could understand

I'm more alive

than I've ever been

here in the garden

of the Gods

consilium III.

it's simple

you have to stop

wasting your loyalty

on someone who neglects you

heartache and soul mate.

I felt like

you were the moment

and I missed it

you were my moment

and I missed you

a very short tale of sadness.

baby, you define sadness

the longer you stay with a man

who refuses to love you

in a way that makes your heart

feel safe

eligible.

single but worthy of love
and willing to wait for it

peace for the soul.

I thought about you last night

but instead of crying or feeling upset

there was this drizzle of peace

that began to hit the surface of my
soul

I made it

without you . . .

I'm much happier

here without you . . .

day drinking.

hurt and hungover

crying Hennessy tears

kill this idea.

death to this idea

that strong women

must sacrifice

their independence

to make weak men

feel comfortable in a relationship

misplacing strength.

just think about it

if you're strong enough

to tighten your grip

and hold on to a relationship

that hurts you . . .

you'll one day

be strong enough

to walk away

toward your peace

and closer to someone better

digital relationships.

heart emojis

from someone

who just wants to use you

I miss your text messages

from the same person

who left you

to deal with your feelings alone

I love yous from someone

who made you hate yourself

for catching feelings

welcome to my generation . . .

when love is hate.

a man who waits
until he destroys your heart
to tell you how much you mean to him
doesn't deserve you

a man who treats you
as if he hates you
only to express how much he loves you
is no longer worthy
of your emotional energy

all ways.

give your heart to a man
who loves you always
in all ways

another illusion.

you were just an illusion
of everything I thought I needed
you were just a lie
pretending to be the truth

December 2nd 2015.

we were strangers
but when I met you
I remembered who you were

I realized that we've always
been in search of each other
searching for a love that only
you and I could create together

I'm blessed to have found you
in this lifetime as well as any other

I love you

too late, despair.

fuck you

for arriving too late

what I felt

now lives in the past

behind the loads of shit

you promised

ill intentions

wrapped in beautiful linen

lies mistaken for truth

a love that felt more like despair

midnight bled into morning.

the more you ignore me

the more detached I feel

silence fills the room

as my heart becomes empty

and the sensation of love begins to
leave my body

being constantly told how good I am

and yet feeling as if I'm not good
enough

taken for granted, mistreated, and/or
neglected

takes a toll on the human psyche

it's draining for the soul

and I don't have much left

I get quiet because I'm tired

I say nothing because my words

are too difficult for you to
comprehend

one day I won't be here

and you'll no longer have my feelings
to disregard

one night you'll sleep without me

and the nightmare of my absence

will keep you up all night

one morning you'll wake up alone

and realize that you lost an entire
future

when I walked away

midday woes.

honestly

I just want the love

I've given you

icebox.

my heart made cold

by your icy insults

emotion no longer present

and so I give you my absence

what are we?

death to the idea

of being loyal

to someone

who refuses to define

the status

of the relationship

death to the idea

of giving your all

to someone

who refuses

to provide you with

what you deserve

observations.

we entertain chaos

in relationships

because we love that feeling

of resolving issues

making up

and being able to successfully

get back to a place of peace

and sometimes

while arguing, fighting each other

we're essentially fighting

for each other

blindsided.

it's almost as if

he encouraged you

to feel something

and as soon as you caught

what you felt was love

you were blindsided

with pain

facing the fact

that you allowed yourself

to feel for someone

who cared nothing for your heart

322 2016.

my heart belongs to you

I know it's not easy loving someone

like me

I have a certain type of tint to my
soul

which makes it more difficult for
others

to see inside

I lived most of my life as a madman,
perfectionist,

and/or tortured artist

obsessed with the details of the things

that I'm passionate about

and this may explain why I obsess over
you

tomorrow makes 27 years on earth for
me

and in all my life

I've never known something so beautiful

and precious

in all my life I've never seen such
beauty in one person

in a world where many

have disappointed me

you are the one person who has never
let me down

I'm grateful for our union as a couple

and our partnership in life

I love you . . .

go-between.

between the pain and the guard
she keeps in front of her heart
is a woman worth fighting for

winter blue.

sometimes sadness
is the only way out

painful is the path
that leads to something better

girls like you II.

the girls

with the most scars

have the greatest stories of strength

2 a.m.

declare victory

don't let him break you

5 a.m.

love her

like you're losing her

March 22nd 2012.

screaming in silence

crying within

while wearing a smile

the sun begins to set

the sky barely lit

caught between the fading light

and darkness

feels like a metaphor

for my life

or even yours

anticipating something better

as it would seem

the impossible is what you're waiting
for

I feel it too

life is a noose

with nothing new

different day

same emotions

false claims of love

filled my heart

all because I kept it open

so much for hoping

so much for trying

living on promises

but they were broken

your lies

my denial

your love

filled with hatred

my eyes

swelling over

crying rivers of deceit

and I hate it

feeling like life is over

but we're alive

we always make it

the next time someone

offers you a love less than yours

you no longer have to take it

so as the sun sets

on my life once again

you and I are not alone

in this moment

we are friends

the free spirit.

you could never cage her
she ran wild in search of freedom
in search of everything she deserved
she belonged to no man
she belonged to herself

722, faith.

I saw an angel for the first time

the very moment

my eyes opened

and witnessed

this brown-eyed

soft-voiced woman

uttering a prayer

that included my name

I saw heaven

in the way her lips moved

I found religion

in the words she spoke

I found faith

in her tone

I know love

because of her

stopped believing.

I followed my heart

in my walk toward you

and somewhere along the way

I lost the most important thing I had

. . . that belief that I deserved more

that belief that maybe you were never
the one

while she sleeps.

the moon whispers your name every
night

my heart pulsates, aching for you
each night

I'm watching you sleep and now I know
what angels look like when they rest
their wings

love unfolds itself during this hour
and me myself, I am most vulnerable
hours before the sun rises

I miss you but you're here, silence
fills the room, my desire for
you . . . so loud

I love you

even during the worst terms, bad
times, not just when things are good

for every bit of this life, I love you

for as long as I live,

I love you

and in the next life, the next time,
my love will remain unchanged

so if my chance of tomorrow never
comes

and my time ends before I awake, let
this be a long-lasting testament of
how much I love you

June 10th 2016.

I don't think you understand
the impact of your ideas and thoughts

mostly negative
leaving your tongue
sitting on your lips
pushed toward my ears
finding their way to my heart
causing ripples in my soul

I can recall the day
or the way
the letters you used
to create words
that would somehow
change my entire life

though not in that
particular moment
it is now evident
as I type these words

it is evident as I sit here

under the moon

sitting on a past

filled with pain

and confusion

or this delusion

that the things you

screamed

or did unto me

passive aggressively

somehow were the truth

or that I deserved them

how wrong were you

and so wrong was I

untitled.

your ex will always try
to reappear
once he sees you wearing
the smile he often destroyed

especially when that smile
is because of someone new

flames in the distance.

there's not enough paint

to cover these walls

where I carved our names

and so as I light this match

tossing it upon this gasoline-filled
room

tonight, what we were

goes up in flames

our love in ashes

our love to dust

more of less.

metaphorically
we died
and everything we were
was just a cold fucked-up memory

you became an afterthought
and I was left to repair
the scars you left upon my existence

your love was a piece of shit
and simply less than I deserved

722 the cure.

in search for a cure

and the universe

prescribed her to me

and on her label it read

"take me . . . twice a day"

yet I often found myself

overdosing on her

fragments of pain.

the pulse of my heart

screams for some sort of change

or indication that things will get
better

I hold on to hope

but I'm losing my patience

I'm losing my mind

I'm losing myself

wet lips and fingertips.

my cold hand

on her warm thigh

silence was our song

this woman

was something rare

the way she created waterfalls

on the tips of my fingers

me for you.

maybe I'm your one

we are one and the same

in search of the same thing

in search of one another

majesty.

she was King

a ruler on her own

not that easy.

so easily

he walked away

don't make it easy for him

to return

mountain high.

and I believe

that she hid her heart

on a peak of the highest mountain

away from those

too weak to make it to the top

the right intent.

you can forgive
without taking them back
and just because you walk away
doesn't mean you no longer care

sometimes love is one-sided
sometimes what you give
gets taken but never returned
and those situations
usually scar the human heart
for a lifetime

it's okay to walk away
from a promise of love
that was broken

it's okay to turn your back
on someone who pushes you away
without concern of what you feel

it's not you
you're not the problem
you had the right intentions
but your love was just given
to the wrong person

still learning love.

don't build your forevers

on the foundation

of temporary people

undivided.

you're not jealous
you're not insecure
you deserve a man
that won't force you
to feel like
you have to compete
with other women

722 days.

put your love

on top of any mountain

and I will climb it

drop your love

into the ocean

and I will find it

this is

my love

for you

February 2015.

while they only wanted
to observe her on her back
I wished to see her on her feet
and as they tore her down
I'd do anything to build her up

I am restless.

your own memories

betray you

becoming silent threats of pain

destroying that bridge

that often leads to peace

the more you remember

the deeper you dig your own

emotional grave

too many, too often.

how many women are told
that they're different, special,
and beautiful yet continue
to get treated like shit
by men who compliment them

several dead ends.

we get together
based upon some fucked-up
shallow reasoning
exchange I love yous
like it's just something to do

we fall into each other
instead of falling in love
in selfishness
we use each other physically
suppressing the urge to actually feel

and then it's finished
it's over before it truly began

how sad is it
that so many of us
are content
with dead-end relations

when he loves.

a man in love

will never pass up

an opportunity

to be in the presence

of the one he loves

a man in love

will never give

the one he loves

any reason to question

his commitment

a man in love

will always choose

the one he loves

without hesitation

or regret

does he love you . . .

poetic apology.

apologize in the form

of pleasure

every stroke

will whisper "I'm sorry"

death all around her.

dead relationships linger
all around her
in the form of gifts
given in hopes of receiving
something in return

love letters written
under the influence of lust
and nothing more

designer bags
as hush gifts
expensive apologies
for getting caught
and pictures
of people she cared for
now strangers
who only remember her
when they want something

death all around her

in the form of everything

she should forget

or throw away

it's no wonder

her future suffers

buried by

the dirty demeaning men

of her past

pain by patience II.

a woman's patience

shouldn't equate to pain

and suffering

just because you know

she'll wait

doesn't mean

you should make her

journal entry.

this morning feels different
there's a slight silence in the air
but my troubles are still here
weighing me down
like a kettlebell sitting on my chest

I went to sleep last night
with this thought
that everything would be okay
once the sun had reached its peak

I should've known
that my pain would grow
fed by late nights of overthinking
and falling asleep after drinking

my soul at war with my heart

my heart at odds with my mind

they tell me each day is filled with
hope

but every day, I feel hopeless

trying to piece together

all the parts of me

that have been broken

sometimes life is hell

and I simply survive the flames

sometimes I feel uncertain

most of the time, I feel afraid

the unknown lurks

in circles

then hides in the darkest corners

in every place that I inhabit

I want to leave

I want to stay

I want to give up

but maybe I should try

most of the time

I'm fighting against myself

I'm fine

but that's a lie

most of the time

we're fighting

scratching and clawing

simply trying to survive

self-replenishing.

don't forget about your magic,
sweetheart

don't forget about the many battles

you've survived

the many obstacles you've broken
through

don't forget about your ability

to see beyond your obstructed view

right now the only one who can provide

what you deserve

is you . . .

angry.

people will upset you
then label you with having
issues with anger

the hopelessness.

I've been suffocating beneath

this idea of a love

that you'll never be able to provide

grave garden.

stop planting yourself

in dead gardens

brown liquor girl.

she was Hennessy

in a teacup

something wild

but safe

someone strong

and beautiful

roses in the summer.

bloodred petals

scattered across the floor

like beautiful fallen angels

roses in a glass vase

filled with murky water

stems drowning

in many ways

these roses represent

what we were

and where we are now

once beautiful

now dying

all of the people.

I think we're all
just trying to survive
the impact
of falling for someone
incapable of catching us

I think we're all
just trying to survive
the death of a relationship
filled with empty promises
and bad intentions

we've been faced
with the task of making sense
of a reality that was really a lie

I am, you are.

I am enough
just not for you

and that's okay

the contradictions.

how can he be interested in you

when he rarely makes an effort

how is it that you call it love

when you always feel

as if he hates you

June 4th 2016.

I wake up to her asleep

lying beside me

I sit and wonder

about what dreams

she's creating

TV playing

whatever movie

we fell asleep to

she's beautiful

me, watching her lips

as she breathes through

I lean in closer

just to whisper

"I love you"

November 2013.

your lover can never

be taken away from you

and if for any reason

he walks away

for someone else

that person never deserved

to be claimed by your heart

ungrateful unworthy.

stop fighting for appreciation

leave the ungrateful

best days.

the best days of your life
are hidden behind
the worst moments
you'll eventually
survive through

most importantly.

quality over quantity

place more importance

on who deserves you

instead of who simply wants you

to be desired is nice

but to be loved is beautiful

a memory.

guard your memories

they last forever

consilium IV.

you shouldn't have to use sex
to get him to pay more attention to you

a New York summer.

the weather in my heart

is changing

as the atmosphere in New York

inches closer to summer

I feel cold

I feel more like winter

an overwhelming silence

surrounds me

so heavy

weighing down on my soul

I'm running out of patience

frustration is the only thing

I've been able to feel lately

disappointment has become the new
normal

as I sit in anticipation of all the
things

that most likely won't occur

mostly the things which

I desire the most

there's this aching in my heart

as I sit here

typing this as a reflection

of what my emotions

would look like

if placed in front of a mirror

I looked into a mirror this morning

and barely recognized myself

as the smile that I so often

use as a mask

has all but melted away

I feel used, I feel overlooked

I feel more and more

like the worst version of myself

and now I know why people change

now I know why someone with the
biggest heart

would rather close themselves off

from the world

now I know what it feels like

to give everything

and be shortchanged

by the person you'd do everything for

the weather in my heart

is changing

I feel cold

life force.

she is life

drink from her

taste her in ways

that make the hair

on the back of her neck stand

touch her as if

you've gone your entire life

without something or someone to hold

love her with the type of force

that causes her legs to tremble

as she willingly arches her back

welcoming you

she is life

drink from her

taste the future

as it drips down

her inner thighs

eulogy.

everything that I do
every memory that I create
is a detail in my eulogy
a proclamation of where I was
and who I became

in morbid humor
satire mostly
we're all just living to die

writing the novel of
our own lives
a book best received
during our funeral
in a room filled with people
who more than likely care
about the story being told

and so I continue to write
until the final draft
until my deadline

leave and loss.

leave and they'll search for you
in everyone else and fail

this is when they'll understand
what they lost

some suggestions.

read more books

drink more water

ignore more texts

say no more often

and put yourself first

as the sun rises.

but haven't you noticed
you're more like the sunrise
not everyone will see value
in your presence
not everyone will wake up
early enough to appreciate
the sight of you
and that's okay

your light
is not for everyone

January 17th.

she was a giver

she had the biggest heart

she was affectionate

she was often taken for granted

she was the one who felt as if she
loved

too hard

she was the one picking up the pieces

of her own heart

in hopes of starting over

after you left her broken

she was the one

you should've married

now she's the one

who will wear my ring

January 18th.

way too often

weak men waste

the energy of a strong woman

new bridges.

bridges will be burned

but stronger ones will be built

upon their ashes

24 hours.

one day your mind

will replace the thoughts

he consumed

one day your heart

will stop mentioning

his name

you have 24 hours

of each and every day

to get over the hurt he caused

take all the time you need . . .

currently you.

too many good women
stuck in unhealthy relationships
waiting patiently for something
that'll never happen

these urges.

most nights

I crave the softness

of her inner thighs

against the sides

of my face

closer to more.

the moral of this story is

I was honest

you lied

and there was nothing left to say

I left you behind

in order to move forward

I walked away

to get closer to something better

portrait 722.

paint me into your future, please

last night I dreamed about my own death

and so I count down to my own demise

things changed the night we met

conversations shared over text

social media flirtation

notifications telling me that you
replied

I don't think you realize

how much that night

changed my life

paint me into your future, please

your words like paint

your actions, the brush

your love the canvas

illustrate me there and help me live

a bit longer

paint me into your future, my love

let me spend whatever time I have left

with you, in your embrace

our faces touching, the points of our
noses

colliding with ease

your eyes are closed but mine are open

I don't want to shut them

in fear of missing something

that I should see

paint me into your future

until we're old and gray

our skin wrinkled by time

the time I thought I'd lose

before you entered the picture

paint me

paint you

paint us, please

more rules.

love her

marry her

and never stop dating her

sometimes, the brave.

sometimes the bravest thing to do
is to finally give up on those
who continue to quit on you

ladylike.

she's ladylike but likes to fuck

and enjoying the act

doesn't make her a whore

she likes what she likes

the specifics are for her to know

loving sex doesn't destroy

a woman's standards

possibly.

maybe she built that wall

in front of her heart

in order to save herself

from the pain

that she's grown familiar with

heightened flames.

there's fire within her
don't try and put it out
just add to it . . .

the right now.

at some point

in your life

you're going to have to start

demanding what you deserve

and be willing to walk away

if what you require

can't be provided

journey toward self.

I later learned
to appreciate the absence
of those who failed to
cherish my presence

alone, through self-discovery
I learned to love myself
even the parts of my soul
that were often overlooked
and taken for granted

as I listened.

conversation leads to old

the past resurfaces unexpectedly

and I'm reminded

of how much of your life I've missed

I'm reminded of how many moments

I wasn't able to be a part of

most of which may never occur again

the girl I know

is someone else at times

different from who others know

and I'm trying to figure out what
version of you

I'm actually getting

and why for some reason

you could only be wild or free, untamed

or slightly reckless

with so many people other than me

. . . the one you love . . . now

watching others almost forget

the happenings of certain events in
your life

as you go back and forth

about a detail they weren't aware of

at the time

"but you were with someone else"

they say

making admissions without any signs

of guilt or regret

as I'm forced to think to myself . . .

what if it were me

what will occur when certain people

from your past

suddenly believe that you were the one

after making you secondary for most

of their lives

those same people

who caused you to easily

shit on whatever relationship

or situation you were in at that

particular moment

then I drift into our past

remembering the fragments

of trust that have been broken

between you and me

the times you've either kept something

from me or went behind my back

to do something you knew would hurt me

some of the same names pop up

as I watch your eyes slowly stare off

into the distance

as you recount what happened

while keeping certain details to
yourself

locked away in secret

just as you often do

talk of exes

the ones I was aware of

or the ones who were never made
important

until that very moment

where you were

the things you did

and all I could do is sit there

in silence and smile

as if it didn't bother me

but I'm human

and I'm in love

trying to figure where I fit

because in that very moment

there was no room for me . . .

cheating is not a skill

it's a handicap

incapable of loving.

you've been dating your self-esteem

when you're incapable of loving
yourself

you'll place your heart in the hands
of those

who are incapable of loving you

eye of the storm.

that's the thing

in order for the heart

to conquer pain

it has to first confront

everything and everyone

who attempted to destroy it

and if your soul

was strong enough

to withstand the winds of betrayal

you'll find peace and clarity

as you look into the eye of the storm

2009.

she'd complain about the mistreatment
and I'd ask her when it started

she stopped coming around
and I'd ask her where she'd been

phone conversations got shorter
the text messages barely came
and I began to think that I'd said
something wrong

I ran into her a few months ago
but I barely recognized her

she dropped something
and as she picked it up
I noticed all the bruises
by her waist and on her back

I wish I would have said something
I saw the hurt in her eyes
but I was always distracted
by her smile

I wish you would have told me
I wish I would have asked
I wish I would have tried harder
to be there
I wish you would have left

this is what I think
every time I visit the cemetery
to see her

all for self.

be good to yourself

you're the only you

you'll ever get

July 13th 2016.

peaks in the distance

rolling mountains for miles

I fell in love with the springs

of Colorado

beginning to end.

it wasn't love
I was just comfortable
with being yours for the moment
and you were just content
with what we were and what we became

no longer lovers
falling asleep apart
living like roommates
and sometimes strangers

where did we go . . .
I barely noticed
what was happening
until it happened

I turned to look
and you weren't there
you came home
but I had already left

these lives matter II.

every time this happens

I see my father

I see my brother

my friends

at times, I see my would-be son

and then I see myself

humanity is a lost art

a lost practice

an endangered idea

as I observe my brothers

my sisters

your mother or your father

being slaughtered

by those who should have kept them
safe

left to be witnessed

by a community already hurting

left to be witnessed

by would-be victims

of inhumanity

disregarded, disrespected

killed, then reduced to a hashtag

because of the color of their skin

stop killing us

girls like you III.

you're patient
and so your heart puts up
with so much shit

you're strong
and so you're able
to hold on
even when you should let go

you're in love
but you're in love
with a lie
filled with empty promises
and betrayal

girls like you
deserve the type of love
that makes you feel secure
and safe within your emotions

girls like you deserve
a love that fills you
to the point at which you overflow
with joy

girls like you
deserve a love
that reminds you
of how rare your existence is

midsummer retrospect.

not everyone you claim
to be close to
is an actual friend
and this becomes more apparent
as progression finds you

those friends become leaves
slowly falling to the ground
as you achieve success

the more your life improves
the less likely
those friendships last

Times Square.

standing in the middle of Times
Square

on a Friday night

just me, my lover, in the middle of it
all

witnessing lost souls in miniskirts

and creeps who only appeal

to any woman inebriated

by dark liquor and loneliness

that used to be me

a child of the night

sending what's-her-name

on a walk of shame

wasting away

in search of something

that turned out to be myself

and there I stood

in the middle of a light show

that seemed more like a shit show

she's unable to walk

twisted filled with drinks

unable to make the right decision

becoming prey

to the hunters in fitted caps

fake jewelry and designer labels

the night bleeds into the morning

and I hope you're drunk enough to
forget

what he won't remember

a night in.

I think I used going out as a
distraction

from the loneliness I felt

but I'd be sitting dead center

in a dark room, drinks flowing

music blaring

feeling more alone than I'd ever been

surrounding myself

with lonely strangers just as lost as me

I don't miss the nights

looking for some stranger to help me
self-medicate

the trauma of having no one to go home
to

or no one to share my life with

sometimes I lie here next to my lover

and think to myself

how good it feels to choose staying in
over

any nightclub and how good it feels

to spend time with someone who actually

deserves mine

the solitude.

there's something beautiful
about the solitude
that settles in your heart
after you've accepted
the imperfect ending
of something you thought
would last

master the task of being alone
take advantage of those silent moments
created by the realization
that the person you care for
is no longer deserving of your effort

consilium V.

save your energy

starve his ego

stop entertaining someone

who amplifies your pain

long distance made short.

I met a girl
who shared the same
sadness as I

glowing skin
a fragile smile
with a brown tint in her eye

we fell in love
before we should have
in love so deep
like ocean's blue

we buried seeds
of what we wanted
something so small
and then it grew

great pain.

the greatest pain

produces

the strongest hearts

the infinite.

she needed nothing
from no one
basking in her own independence
comfortable within her strength

she was the type of woman
who made weak men uneasy
she was the type of woman
you couldn't flatter
with a simple compliment

because she was more
than what met the eye
as her true value
was always infinite

to Frank.

more than a father

you are King

guardian of the woman

who later became my Queen

I am grateful

for your hands

because you held her

I am grateful for your mind

because you taught her

and I am grateful for your heart

because the love you gave

is the love she's given unto me

a Sunday afternoon.

a relationship without loyalty
is like a body with no soul

July 2nd 2016.

a man who waits
until he hurts you
to tell you how much
you mean to him
doesn't deserve
your emotional energy

change the locks
to your heart's door
and move forward
with your life

rose garden.

the garden in her heart
is filled with dead roses
different versions of love stories
that seem more like nightmares

lessons in the form of heartache
lessons in the form of everything
that would otherwise destroy her

but even though it hurts
and even when it falls apart
there she stands
refusing to give in

a crown made of flowers
a smile filled with strength

he can't love you.

you can't force a man
to see you
for who you truly are
when he's blinded
by his own immaturity

you can't force a man
to provide the type of love
he's incapable of giving

you'll never have to force
the type of love you require
with a man who deserves
to be a part of your life

travel with or without.

see the world

with someone

who is honest

loyal and considerate

in terms of your feelings

see the entire world

with someone

who truly loves you

and if you can't find that

see the world by your damn self

the unfortunate truth.

what's unfortunate
is that we place more value
on our feelings
than our bodies
when both are just as valuable

people would rather catch
something that can't be cured
than catching feelings
and as much as I'd like to laugh
at this logic
it's honestly just sad

building your own peace.

in order to find peace

you must begin to say no

to anything or anyone

who doesn't deserve a yes

and you must do this always

without apology

and with confidence

the rules.

I was taught by a woman
to never allow my woman
to feel threatened by another woman

I was taught by a woman
to never allow a woman
that isn't my woman
to feel more important
than the woman I love

these are the rules
unbreakable, these commandments
taught to me by a woman
value the teachings from a woman

consilium VI.

refuse to be someone's hobby

you are not just something to do

heaven, whiskey, and her.

cranberry and whiskey

heaven in a tall glass

as I struggle to type these words

on the laptop she bought me

she's just sitting there

phone in hand

Veronica Mars playing in the background

and all I can think about

is the way that green dress

hugs her thighs in a way

that really speaks to my fantasies

with clean hands

and a dirty mind

I struggle with sober thoughts

as my thinking sinks

into a pool of liquor

my first book is a bestseller
my second book finds life in June
and all I can think about is
what type of ring
I should buy her

she's been working out more lately
and her fingers are slightly thinner
so the size that I have
may no longer be valid

all this while sipping
cranberry and whiskey
I'm in heaven
with this glass, next to her
I am one lucky man

the ending.

what if this is the last book I ever
write

what if every passage or poem

printed on these pages

are simply my way of saying good-bye

without actually realizing it

this beautiful journey

reaching some sort of stop

which causes me to unpack

the heaviness that has often

filled my heart

weighing me down

causing me to sink

into an abyss

what if these what-ifs

become a reality

and my voice is silenced

fingers unable to type

mind no longer able

to think the things

that you relate to so much

if this is that

and that is this

thank you . . .

thank you for giving me

your undivided attention

thank you for allowing these words

to touch the innermost parts of your
soul

this is where we leave it all behind

this is where we bury the pain of our
past

this is where it ends

thank you and good-bye . . .

maybe next time I'll . . .

<u>index.</u>

whiskey words & a shovel III

Andrews McMeel Publishing
a division of Andrews McMeel Universal
1130 Walnut Street, Kansas City, Missouri 64106

www.andrewsmcmeel.com

18 19 20 21 22 RR2 10 9 8 7 6 5

ISBN: 978-1-4494-8459-0

Library of Congress Control Number: 2016934683

Editor: Patty Rice

Designer, Art Director: Diane Marsh

Production Editor: Erika Kuster

Production Manager: Cliff Koehler

attention: schools and businesses

Andrews McMeel books are available at
quantity discounts with bulk purchase for
educational, business, or sales promotional
use. For information, please e-mail the Andrews
McMeel Publishing Special Sales Department:
specialsales@amuniversal.com.